STILL BREATHING

More or less

Margy Hillman

Hillman Consulting, LLC

Copyright © 2021 Hillman Consulting LLC

All rights reserved

The characters and events portrayed in this book are fictitious. Any similarity to real persons, living or dead, is coincidental and not intended by the author.

No part of this book may be reproduced, or stored in a retrieval system, or transmitted in any form or by any means, electronic, mechanical, photocopying, recording, or otherwise, without express written permission of the publisher.

ISBN-13: 9798673332436
ISBN-10: 1477123456

Cover design by: Art Painter
Library of Congress Control Number: 2018675309
Printed in the United States of America

CONTENTS

Title Page
Copyright
Introduction
What Lies Beneath?   1
Death and Plastic Surgery   3
We R The Vampires   4
A Slant   5
Color me?   6
Inside Out   8
A Love Song   9
Stop Whining, J. Alfred   10
Pandemic morning   12
I Am Open   13
Lagoon   14
When we were poor   16
As a child   17
After the Fire   19
Fee Fi Fo Fum   20
Change of State   21
Wolves at the Door   22
While I cook dinner   24

Before I Forget	25
citizen's arrest	26
My Children & Theirs	27
Knee of my day	28

INTRODUCTION

If you put my brain into a giant aluminum pan and covered it in tap water and boiled it for a few hours and then turned the flame to simmer and then let this pungent stew boil down to syrupy gunk and scraped a spoon (not wooden) around the edges and blew on it till it was almost cool. Well, that's how my poetry tastes.

WHAT LIES BENEATH?

You may find me
Quietly drowning
Weighed down by lies
Anchored by expectations

At the center of my lies
Are a thousand truths I cannot tell
Because
I am troubled by monsters and demons
Better suited to gothic tales

Do you believe in the devil?
Has he sat by the side of your bed?
Smelling of cheap gin and cigarettes
Sweaty and loose jawed
Has he spoken to you?

"Shhhhhh," he says
"Don't wake the baby.
Your mama will be mad. So mad."

So you go inside your head and count to 34
And when you come back
You smell him on you and you vomit
all over the floor in the hall
Then your mama does wake up and she is mad. So mad.
Clean it up yourself, she says.
So you do

MARGY HILLMAN

DEATH AND PLASTIC SURGERY

When you get to a certain age
You start thinking a lot about two things
Death and plastic surgery
I'm not sure which one is most significant
Probably plastic surgery which hopefully
Is more immediate

Calculate the time spent staring into the mirror lifting up the skin
over your cheekbones
Tucking up the skin under your chin
Raising your eyebrows and widening your eyes
Ah yes
We need the scalpel you say
And maybe a few star wars type lasers to smooth and lift the skin
all over your body
And it wouldn't hurt to have some permanent makeup
Your lips could use plumping and a more definite outline
Ack and get rid of the freckles and the age spots and the bruising
Errant hairs would be good to have gone
And if we're going to all this trouble how about a boob job and
a butt lift and a tummy tuck

And then you start thinking about death
What I really want is not to die
Is there a doctor who can promise that?
Then I'm in!

WE R THE VAMPIRES

Do you remember when the sun was good?
Light and warmth
Central character in photosynthesis
Gold label source of Vitamin D
Fellow traveler of gods and goddesses

We shun the poor guy now
Slather on sunscreen
Wear wide-brimmed hats

Replace him with
High doses of D3 and anti-depressants
Angry at his steady vigilance
"Another day of deadly heat," the weather news alarms

(Altho as the sun might point out we were the ones that destroyed the stratosphere)

A SLANT

Words
label stuff so we know if something is good or bad
they give words
a slant

like sexual abuse
Sexual
Who doesn't love that?
I mean it's sex, darling.

Abuse
seems all the sweeter
when married to sex

In fact the rapist comes out pretty shiny

COLOR ME?

Color me what?
When I was growing up I was considered too white
It was a time when white people – particularly women – wanted to be tan
Not brown mind you but tan in which case it was best to have blonde hair just to make it clear that under the color you were white
Me I just burned

Color is marvelous, darling
Except for certain colors
Like brown, black, and red
It's really not that clear when you think about it
I mean some black people are tan or brown and some white people are dark
Like my brother who is brown but whose clients are happy when they learn he is white

When I was in first or second grade my mom let me have a birthday party and she let me invite a few of the kids in my class and so of course I did and was so excited my first real birthday party
But when my best friend came to the door with her mother
My mother looked at me and said how could you do this?
And I just stared at her because she knew I had invited Vida but till this moment to her Vida was a little girl
a little white girl
And she told Vida's mom they couldn't come in because they were colored
And she shut the door in their faces
And I cried and cried because she was my best friend and I could

hear her cry and that still makes me so sad

And I think how Vida's mom must have felt so powerless and angry protective of Vida and I hope she got her an ice cream and told her not to cry that some people are weighed down by their hatred

And what started this conversation in my head is that color and hatred go hand in hand in this country
This is how we organize our hatred of people who are
not like us
(unless we can find other ways like religion, or gender, or height, or education, or age, or domicile, or food, or smell, or grades; there are a million ways to sort people into them and us
and color is tricky because it's just the reflection of light so you have to teach your kids to see the color you think you see)

The physics of color is easy in comparison to the color of hate

INSIDE OUT

Between the neural synapses
I am the fire
That jumps here to there
Creating pathways
One wrong jump
One false leap
Angels on a pinhead
Paradise or
Dirt

A LOVE SONG

Layer me
Cheek to my cheek
Breath to my sigh
Skin against skin
Hand against heart
Lay me
To rest
Your hand on my breast

Layer me your mind to mine
Synapse to synapse
Free to divine
Breath against breath
Light to my day
Lay me
To dream
Your hand to my heart

Layer me your soul to mine
Meta to physics
No me without you
Particle to particle
No in between
And into this parentheses
Leap my love
Leap

STOP WHINING, J. ALFRED

I too grow old, old man
You with your trousers
And the cuffs that you've rolled
But you hide your fear in the language of pedants and fools
So literary the oxygen so thin

Come, sink to my level

My skin might look like a sweater
But I'm not getting old
I'm just getting better

The serum I slather on my skin
Warns me to avoid expressions
As long as I can

My teeth they too age
So I buy strips made by Crest
And apply them before smiling so I'll look my best

I sweat like a pig so I only wear black
And all of my clothes are designed
To cover my front and my back

I've noticed that when I walk down the street
People coming my way
Don't part or move aside

I'm invisible

At last

I like my wine red
I like my wine white
And sometimes I use it to get through the night

I sleep with my Kindle instead of a man
Because the men my age
Want objects a little newer so they can live forever

But listen
Prufrock, my friend,
When I call to the sea
The mermaids swim up and they call to me

When death comes to get me
I'm refusing to leave
I'll play in the sea foam
As it comes and it goes

PANDEMIC MORNING

Every morning at 4:30 am,
The coyotes come out to kill
I don't like the sound but still I keep my window open

Sometimes they stay out and sit
under the trees on the village green
Or wander down the streets and alleys

This early there are only a few of us out
Breathing
Some with masks, some without

Birds chase each other from tree to tree
Are they mating?
Snails hurry across sidewalks leaving silver trails
And rollie-pollies peak out from blades of grass

Bushes are ripe with bees
Buzzing happily, defying their decline
Crows fly above
The flapping of their wings makes a solid whap
As they push the air down then up
And rise

The boss crow sits tall upon the street light
Cawing out commands

I AM OPEN

Here and there
Signs of spring
Tiny green leaves and pink buds
Ready to blossom

I face the sun
Her light lifts my spirits
I sit and write
A scrivener
The clock is ticking

Then comes
Night cold and moonless
Its chill like dry ice
Dare I slip into sleep?

The labyrinth of my dreams
Wearies me but
I wake at dawn
Wrestle from sleep
The sky moves from dark to light
Its muted greys and rose and lemon yellow

Raise the day

LAGOON

The path to the lagoon
Runs downhill
Dry and covered with gravel
And coyote dung

It parallels the freeway and
As my dog and I traverse its narrow and steep path
I watch drivers
Pick their noses
In traffic jams
So dense
The cars move more slowly than we do

Closer to the lagoon
I smell water and dirt
The gravel gives way to loamy sand
And the trees begin

Tall grey eucalyptus
And grey green sage
Line the path

At the edge of the lagoon
The trees lie helter skelter
As if in some drunken
Stupor
They have fallen and they can't get up

The disarray is a comfort

To my landscaped life
I like the clutter

At the lagoon
Ducks slip in and out of the water
Quietly provoking my dog

And then a skinny egret looks up and
Takes flight
His wings spread
And with graceful aerodynamics
He rises

Rises

Into the air

And then

Away

WHEN WE WERE POOR

When we were poor
We lived in an apartment building
Close to the freeway

In fact I could do a traffic report from my bedroom window
I grew used to the sound of the cars swooshing by
The horns and screeching of metal against metal
The cacophony was my nighttime lullabye

Now I have plenty
And I live in a house on a hill
Overlooking the ocean

I have found that
The ocean sometimes sounds like the freeway
Waves the traffic
Seabird squawks the near collisions
This cacophony a machine in the garden

AS A CHILD

On the weekends my dad and mom would take us to Mexico to go to the beach
Because my father didn't like crowds and did like to sit and drink all day while we kids ran down the beach and my mom sat with baby Mo

The sea took care of us
I don't know why
Six children racing along the foam edges of waves
She kept us safe as we wandered
In her shallow waters
With sand sharks and
Man o' wars

We skipped flat green and grey stones across her surface
Jumped into waves to save conch shells and sand dollars

We explored her reefs
Found refuge in her caves and hollows
Dead seagulls and baby seals
Carnage that told us she could be cruel

Her sandy beaches
Creating underwater rivers that
ran back to her, taking her victims to quiet graves

I pretended I was the mother of my
Sisters and brothers
Making sure that we stayed in flock
We were unafraid

MARGY HILLMAN

Except to return

Were we lonely?
Not really
The ocean kept us without complaint

Heading back as the sun went down
I knew my father would have moved from beer to gin
And the monster would be sitting on his haunches
Waiting for
the kill

But for the moment
The crash of the waves on the sandy shores
Were soothing
As a lullabye
And we were safe
As the tide moved in and then out
In and then out

AFTER THE FIRE

After the fire
The forest was more spacious
Trees stood awkwardly apart

Naked and
Burned from the inside out

Like a house empty of furniture
Family gone
Waiting

FEE FI FO FUM

The air and ground pulsate
He comes
Leering

Come on, honey

I am everywhere everything

Open to me and I will take you make you
Mine

Tired
I lie down
And disappear

One day
I will fly

CHANGE OF STATE

When summer turned to fall
I was there

Smelled it tasted it
Crisp leaves under foot

Air heavy with grasses and fog and the sky the sky
Its brilliant blue faded to grey

Sun austere and removed
Moon fat and yellow as an egg yolk

Cicadas on the hillside
Their sound shrill
As an owl swoops over the streetlight and away

I walked in and out of shadows
Listening
To mice and squirrels scatter
The round white tails of rabbits bobbed out of sight
Into the dark

WOLVES AT THE DOOR

Wolves at the door
They would eat my heart
They howl
But
My door is double locked

And
I stand pressed against it
I can feel their hot breath against my cheek

Open up they howl
Open up

But
I have opened before
I know this game

I have lost my heart before
To the moon
To the tender doe who stands still in her light

Lost it to the wild lupine
To the blue dusk

I have given it to hollow men
Who never asked

But I have never run with wolves
Who would eat my heart
My heart

Who would eat my heart
Should I open

WHILE I COOK DINNER

While I cook dinner
I listen for the geese

Long before their jagged formation
Cuts across my backyard sky
I hear them barking
Like seals or dogs
Or noisy children coming in from recess

I imagine that they gossip about this and that
As they move in a pixelated V
Season to season
Place to place
Some circadian clock

Ticking ticking ticking
Can this be wild?

BEFORE I FORGET

I decided to start the year today
Winter sun gentle
Shadows hide the chill

The canyon path is dry
The mud hardened and full of bike tracks and paw prints
I forget to look for snakes

People
Walking in groups, chatting softly in words I don't understand
But in a language I do know

Slivers of light on the horizon
As if God had pulled up the curtain hiding heaven

(Which I would love to believe in so I could go there

Later)

(Much later)

At my corner the ocean and canyon meet
And wind ruffles my hair
Faith rises

CITIZEN'S ARREST

The wind
bursts up canyon walls
Criss-crosses alleys
Runs along curbs and tumbles into intersections and makes left turns without signaling

MY CHILDREN & THEIRS

I may have to leave you without a proper ending
No long good-byes

But know
Each of you
Gave
Me life
Not the other way around

I see you
I know you each of you and yes I love who you were are will be

Make your choices
Change your mind
Dare to make mistakes

Love until your heart breaks
And then mend it back again

A mother's love is savage
Death cowers before me
And so I will reach across
to you
Wild and deep we are forever
And
Do not cry my babies
Because I am always here

KNEE OF MY DAY

Knee of my day
Genuflect
Bone touches dirt
Sun sinks out of sight

I cross myself
North south west east

Between day and night
Time stops to take a breath

Amen is not in my nature
But I will take this blessing

Made in the USA
Columbia, SC
18 October 2022